Shotgun-House Guitar

a collection of poems and musings

Gregory Powell

Broad Wing Press

Shotgun-House Guitar: A Collection of Poems and Musings

© Gregory Powell 2023

ISBN: 978-1-938373-47-3
LCCN: 2023945170

© Broad Wing Press 2023

Cover Design: "Autumn Lamp Guitar Player"
© 2023 Romare Bearden Foundation/Licensed by VAGA at Artists Rights Society (ARS), NY

"… come celebrate with me that everyday something has tried to kill me and has failed." –

Lucille Clifton

Dedication

I dedicate this collection to my parents, Franklin Powell Sr. (a/k/a Red), and my mother, Florence Williams Powell for creating a joyful life for me and my siblings (Deborah, Franklin, Patricia, Jewel, and Pandora).

Appreciation

I thank the Romare Bearden Foundation for the cover art. I thank my poetry editor, Vanessa Turner Burke, who has the patience of Job. I thank Dr. Estrelda Alexander, President of William Joseph Seymour Foundation and executive Editor of Broad Wing Press . I thank the professors at Morehouse College for "seeing" me. I thank my mentor, poet Bruce Smith of Syracuse University, and Dr. Jacqueline Rouse who transitioned during COVID; thank you for inviting me to your table to break bread and wonder. Holy Spirit, continue your work in me.

Finally, I thank *Progressive* magazine for first publishing "Combing My Dad's Hair" and "Stop and Frisk" in their February/March 2024 edition. Also, I thank the *African American Review* for previously publishing the poem "The Interview" in Volume 44, Number 3, Fall 2011.

Table of Contents

Combing My Father's Hair 1
Ode to Bell-Bottom Jeans 2
Villanelle at 57 3
Stingy Brim 4
No-Knock Warrants 6
Father Theorem 7
Making Grade in Memphis 8
A Villanelle for William Matthew 9
Temple of the Tooth 10
Lee Morgan 11
He Measures 13
The Egg Sellers 14
Rhythm Hound 15
Flysheet 16
Villanelle for James Brown 17
What is Grace? 18
Malcolm X 19
Pitching Quarters 20
An Elegy for Clara 22
Bebop 24
Villanelle for My Morehouse Brothers 26
Lindy Hop 27
After Reading James Baldwin's *Open Letter* to his Nephew 28
Zoot Suit 30
Smallpox Blanket 32
War Room 33
Widow Maker 34
Retort 35
Uncle JP 36
Cow-Foot Soup 37
The Interview 38
Tiger's Milk 39
St. Bluesman of Eads, Tennessee 40

The Accomplice 41

St. Improvisation Speaks for the First Time 42
America 43
A Reliable Bridge 44
Jim Crow 45
The Potter 46
Stop-and-Frisk 47
Rooster Blues 48
A Loaf of Bread 50
James Brown 51
Flophouse 52
Dutch Nigger 53
Osceola 54
Villanelle Dressed in Blues 55
Phineas Newborn Jr 56
Phineas' Bones & Blues 57
The Alchemist 58
Art Blakey 59
The Reluctant King 61
Regret 62
A Moment to Dress 63
Expendables 64
Turn Your Plate Down 65
Liturgy 66
Gluttony 67
The Idiot Who Would be King 68
American Proverbs 69
Statue of Liberty Meets Bessie Smith for Sunday Brunch 71
Steel-Toed Boot: 1965 72
Requiem of a Lightweight 73
Ali in Full Bloom 75
Villanelle for the New York Stock Exchange 76
Sonnet for the Boxing Bumble Bee 77
Shade Tree 78
A Lament for Lightnin' Hopkins 79

Vanity 81
Please 82

Hermeneutic	83
American Theology	85
Elegy for Howlin' Wolf	86
St. Hummingbird	88
Struggle	89
House Money	90
Critical Race Theory	91
Desperation	92
George Floyd	93
Fall Face First	94
Voting Rights	96
Shotgun House Guitar	97

Combing My Father's Hair

For Franklin Powell Sr. (a/k/a Red)

Posting Up between buckshot & paternal
bloom. I stand behind our kitchen chair.
Where Dad is seated with pockets of
Charm and loose change. No hard start.
Though standing only 5'8" you'd think I'm
the Center in this NBA coliseum of spoons,
pans, pots & jack-legged barbering skill: His is
my first head, a globe framed by Field Holler
& endless grace. Tender-headed, he squirms in
the chair. As if he's a catfish dangling from my lure
& line. Confession: I'm tender-headed too.
Scratch my head with a comb's teeth & I wail.

Howlin' Wolf, salty & perfumed, thunders from
Dad's 8-track tape, edging us in sage & loam.

Ode to Bell-Bottom Jeans

For Patricia Edwards

When you know better you do better.
Don't have to own a Bible to walk upright.
Tell me how long the train been gone?

We don't keep score, but we accept coupons
To be used for a more convenient groove
Cuz when you hear better you do better.

After we'd walked nautical miles, stronger
With each clip of our red platforms. Posting
Up, waiting for the next train headed to Biloxi.

Standing on 5-inch stacks in a gust of Mississippi
Shake & Skank. Polyester shirts cleave to our rib cages,
Flagging the sermon "Know Better – Do Better Blues."

Bells from the sanctified church extend our hour.
Our posse of bell-bottom jeans chill out & lean into
Al Green's tenor, preaching our train is long, long gone.

We stand in a blast of bell-bottom jeans & Afro Sheen.
Celebrating our diverse flavors in a hoop of joy & sunshine
Cuz we know: when you know, you know what you know.

We dress to impress, to fit in, but we ain't no clown show
Lost in a flora of velvet lapels & rotgut swiped from our fathers.
Whose train has been gone for so long they no longer linger.

Nothing's better: elephant bells below our alabaster knees.
We can motorize our five-inch platforms to run a decathlon
From our parents' front porches to school to this holy moment.
Once we catch that train, we will slow-walk it back to Memphis.

Villanelle at 57

I'm not the *Thief* in this Temple.
Some people love you; others hate you.
Christ's love is very simple, Simple.

Mom says, "Be humble as a Lamb."
Pop: "You're a Black Lion—now Roar!"
Colored people ain't Thieves in this Temple.

Jim Crow asks, "Why not live to be a model?
Why not be a tribute for your race?"
O, Jesus' love = just that simple, Pimple.

Jim's question is worse than shameful.
I am who I am and nobody else.
Who are the Thieves in our Temple?

All ground I walk belongs to me.
Test my faith on my own timetable.
Jesus, His love is just that simple, Pimp.

While Jim, parboiling in idiot juice, pops his pimples,
We lean back on our faith & drift on hope
Because we're not the Thieves in this Temple!

I am who I want to be: two dimples,
Hazel eyes of June seeking light.
Christ's love is just that simple.

Thieves hunger for our spiritual gifts.
Where the Living Christ removes & renews.
A Temple built *not* by human hands on flextime.
Yes, Jesus' love is simply that simple.

Stingy Brim

For Henrietta Lacks
August 1, 1920-October 4, 1951.

A pork-pie hat seals Lester Young in a
sweep of syncopated shout & wrench.

After he'd dipped his big toe in
Bessie Smith's cache of pot liquor & liberation.

Now, he mouths zoot-suit zoom & fedora
swing across a reed, flagging his big feet

To unchartered roads of "This Here The Blues!"
and endless reams of "Give It To Me Straight!"

The only light I swing shapes & creases
the crown of my stingy brim on my soft

Head. Narrowing my brim to persistent
prospect & improvisation's holy bloom.

America, we've given you our best …
We are not the thieves of *this* union.
**

Blood cousin of zoot-suit code &
A milliner's golden needle. Lester
was born a grown man of Swing's
Melodic Rebellion & "Lean on Love."

What a Man! Free to angle bebop's
brim down to acknowledge the ladies in
the front row, which pitches his brim up in
the back, snatching stingy breezes on stage.

I can't pivot a brass ax from New York rooftops
to a single Blue Note. A leather flask of
Cognac & "We Just Getting Started, Baby"
Packed in a brown paper bag, headed to Memphis.

Lester, king of telescopic crowns & felt …
We cast our brims at your holy feet.

***

In a kitchen of *head-cutting* sessions.
With congregants of master skill & stream.

Fellowshipping with Black brothers & sons
who cannot create without stingy brims

Resting on their bopping crowns: Rookie
figuring & blow bow to hours of dogged

fingering-and-repeat. Where architects
perfect a throne to 'field shout and holler.'

Lester's ax won't cut a ripe tomato. Until
parboiled in hot-kitchen jam sessions. Where

skill, form and "Check this out!" rub against
the buckle-up & dare of rebellion's blast.

This ain't your mom's or pop's kitchen—
but a house of shift & acceleration.

No-Knock Warrants

Eddie Floyd knocks on our front doors. As if
he owns Stax Records & the Memphis
skyline too. Calling my dad by his first
Name, pouring Dad cups of coffee & Respect.

On Saturday mornings Floyd's tenor rattles
our tin roof & windowpanes. Then, unscrews
mason jars holding a Black man's fury
& discontent with the hush of illegal

Search & night raids. Ask Breonna Taylor
if blows of No-Knock & Disrespect respected
her holy bed of innocence. Under
a roof she owned & paid good money for?

Enough marijuana chitchat & police
lies: Stop killing innocent colored people!

Father Theorem

I did not know
Your words
Could stroll
On paper?

Or that you do not
Have to remove
Your shoes before
You haunt a page?

Making Grade in Memphis

You shot bones with your buddies before graduating to the backrooms of red-hot/shake joints. Navigated for a Gambler's Purse of Gold, Good Luck & Good Looks. Stood in a loop of sharecroppers (twice your age), betting their last lame dollars that lady luck would smile on them. Or, at least, blow sweet kisses until they sank onto their camel knees. Others kicked dirt from bunion-split brogans. July's fury flushes, ripens you. As the *Houseman* plants his leather horn in the center of that desperate ring, drops dice down the horn's leather throat, draws small circles on the concrete floor with the horn & screams like a scalded banshee: "Bet don't bitch! Bet don't bitch! Bet don't bitch! Bet don't bitch! Bettin' men bet. Watchin' men watch. Bettin' men bet. Watchin' men watch the sun go down." "I got two dollars." "I'll fade your two. Got two more in my shoe." "I got five." "I'll fade your five. Your five's alive." Then dice tumble over one another (like clumsy lovers in a potato sack), down the horn's throat. You think *seven* and the dice face seven. Think *eleven* and the dice face ...

Villanelle for William

For William Matthew Jackson

A dollar beats a dime any day.
I should have paid attention.
Speak up! What did you say?

If time required us to prepay
I probably wouldn't have tasted 20
Cuz dollars beat dimes anyway.

I slow-drag my hollow bones to a runway
Where those of us who've lived beyond
Fifty speak up cuz we know what to say.

In my teens I was lips & *shock*, halfway
Between insolence and its first cousin:
"You know dollars beat dimes every day?"

Then, in my early 20s, when I started to pay
My own way. I had to face time in its eye.
Cause time is the boss & knows what to say.

Now "thank you" paves my superhighway:
Where "patience," tightly fits my hips/thighs,
Knows a dollar beats a dime any day.

If you the same fool at 60 in your day-to-day
As you were in your ill-informed teens, my friend,
Keep quiet! Who'd listen to what you have to say.

In a flora of blue denim & disco wordplay,
I have finally found my center & my joy.
I earn & pocket dollars & dimes every day.
Protest for our voiceless—that's our way.

Temple of the Tooth

A universe of soft pockets & gums
Pummel griskin, iron & curiosity.

Nothing escapes this ivory machine,
Flashing 32 knives of *crunch & dare*.

Nothing. Not the hardtack of hunger
Or its deadly first cousin, isolation.

Nor gluttonous fear crawling his gut,
A Bengal tiger searching for prime rib.

Republicans, loosening white belt buckles,
Inch by insidious inch, munch deceit.

They eat the hopeful & brave for breakfast
'Til their bellies balloon greasy gases.

In their jawline—between mercy & sacrifice—
Resides no root of human compassion.

Lee Morgan

When his mother carried him seven months
She dreamed a flugelhorn then a trumpet
Grew inside her, replaced her ribs with brass
Valves, keyed to compress pain & blow survival.

The morning Lee's head crested, she'd dreamed
Her right hip was a French horn and her left?
A trumpet boiled in a callaloo of new greens
& polished with Father Divine's handkerchief.

Never imagined the tiger milk of
Defeat would sour your stomach so quick.
That disaster would crease your slacks &
Grease the brass lips of your holy trumpet.

Sampling *greater*—that's why your mom
Released you into this cold world, early.

**

Swinging hard bop with thirty-three candles
on a jelly cake. His daddy counted
Only three-fifths a man but he'd wrestled
Jim Crow to the ground, stood on his back, smiled.

His daddy's gusto piped power into Lee's
Gnarly arms & thready legs in New York's
Gutter & grime. As drug's allure snatches
Lee by the throat, squeezes until he falls.

Forgets his horn's name. Ignores the swift kick
Of Imagination's help & holy appeal.
Pisses away opportunity's heft
into a bucket of chitterlings & loss.

Lee's first name becomes addiction & last
Name tries to drown him, but he changes keys.

***

His brass phrases seat us in a bloomy
Room of repose & interpretation.
Opens a door for tin-eared folk like me
To reflect upon grace's sacred hour.

When Lee is not polishing holy stones
For heaven's floor, when he is not unpacking
Tins of melody from his trumpet's lair,
Or sweeping the front porch of *tried and true*,

Lee murmurs brackish mouthfuls of *This Here
Bebop!* into creation's valved heart, salvaged
From Noah's rain-swollen Ark & B.B.
King's perfect pitch—while stroking Lucille.

Lee bows before John Coltrane's "Blue Train,"
A splendid church of light & eternal bloom.

He Measures

His words, never ever by the mouthful.
Verbs alone would make a mausoleum
Of his ivories & square jawline.
Ask Dizzy Gillespie, whose blues
Honed a kingdom of honeyed
Reverence into the mandible & maxilla
Of his trumpet. Ask him—*if* you like truth.

No. No. There are loftier loners
(Where rats & roaches gamble
For the moon & dinner scraps).
This little colored girl, for instance.
Proclaiming her Blackness
In bell-bottoms & corn rolls from Ghana.

Resting between novels & fierceness
She takes holy moments to strike a pose—
On the corner of "You Aint Seen Nothing Yet"
& her dad's steaming bowls of dumplings.
(Yes, she's a daddy's girl & she knows it).
"Flower of Judah." "Thunder in a bottle."

The Egg Sellers

For Jesse Dixon

Al Green's Soul unspools from a bulky 8-track tape
        whose plastic housing of libation & liberation

lash Memphis juke-joints, churches & schools
        to a lay-away of late payments & penance.

Green's tenor steadies our egg truck between
        the yellow lines of country roads & our

morning plan to sell hot-house eggs in an
        endless loop of footwork & thunder-shout.

We hawk single yolks from our library
        of know-how, wilt & egg-head defiance.

With each egg sold the axels on the truck
        save one grunt for next week's tow & roar.

Double yolks—fetching a quarter a carton—
        Slowly proof us to work a grown man's grind.

Rhythm Hound

The acoustic guitar (what my teacher calls a "poor man's cello") leans in the corner, listless, without one string to its name. As a boy, I'd pressed my ear to its sound hole (a rhythm hound even then) & listened for any stray notes left rattling inside its hollow body. Pressed my chapped lips to its six spaghetti strings, hoping left-over blues left on the strings would lube my lips. Would surrender its raw language, its survival notes & lust for life. This guitar had been passed through the hands of four generations of family men; they couldn't carry a tune in Howlin' Wolf's tin bucket, but they would write your name in the sky (above the rooftop of your shotgun house) every time they'd strum this guitar with pearl nails.

I pluck elementary blues in my acoustical-starved world because I can't really truly play. Just broke that last string this past hour. For me, a bridge is meant to be crossed on two feet—not primed from a sound hole rimmed in rosewood & ripe regret. I am hollow inside. Press your ear to my navel—do you hear some safe rambling rose blues? Then, I flipped my acoustic over on my lap & slap out a baseline with my left hand. Tap out an alternating rhythm with my free hand that any hound with a sorry nose could follow: "I woke up this morning—the same thing on my mind. I say, I woke up this morning with the same roaming around in my mind. If you were not a friend of mine. You listening? I tell you, woman, if you were not a friend of my mind. I would leave quicker than you could blink. Pack my leather clutch & leave quicker than you could blink your pretty brown eyes. But you make me want to reach the sky. With you by my side, I can own the sky. Let's stop all this foolishness—find our new way. I say, cut out all this foolish talk—celebrate our own way. Before I'd talk, you knew what I was gonna say. Before you thought it, I was on my way to do it."

Flysheet

Every flapping tongue seeks an ear to hustle,
        regardless if the ear is fleshed or tin-armored.

Steeping in the cartilage of marketing
        & ephemera-blast, each tongue loves itself.

Kings of tactical warfare & flypaper,
        human tongues can strip a tree of its bark

& debone low-budget/salty chitchat
        until it screams "Uncle!" or implodes.

Try this before you load, shoot & reload
        your mouth of lies & satanic guano:

Rinse your mind with Ella's *call-and-response*.
        then set your mouth in sweet basil & kindness.

Join me! Engage in verbal healing,
        erasing airborne slights of tongue & groove.

Villanelle for James Brown

The truth ain't no chump but a *real* man:
My Pop and my uncles validated me.
Real faith grows stronger in its own brainpan.

I am only a man formed from purpose & clay.
Speaking words softened in the mouths of kin.
Truth ain't no chump but a full-grown man.

James Brown was the *real deal*. Not a doorman
For rock 'n' roll. Opened his arms, his wingspan
Eclipsed all but faith's squall from Augusta's brainpan.

When I confront Jim Crow he runs, screams like a banshee.
With tender feelings, rotten (*"critical race theory hurts us"*).
Truth is no chump & churns restrictive covenants into zero & huff.

Brown knew segregation wanted to strangle him, and own
Every blue note spiraling from his mother's hips to the sky.
Is your faith growing stronger every day in your brainpan?

Brown, thank you for tamping down (*with your Good Foot*)
The ignorance spiraling this country's trellis of privilege cause
The truth ain't no mark with no last name but a two-fisted man.

Now I write & unpack unethical notions with an eagle's wingspan
& predatory eyes for the foolish, idol worshippers without hearts.
I can feel faith growing deeper and stronger in my brainpan.

Truth ain't no fool but speaks in blood & stone.
Debones hypocrisy to its birth & demonic brew.
Brown studied & cracked your code: Your DNA
Is what demons feast on & thrive in your brainpan.

What is Grace?

She sports Tina Turner legs,
        caramel & nutbush-muscled.
She begins by slipping a right foot
        into her ancient house slipper,
Sown from pig's ear & clover;
        the sow's bristles begin to petrify.
She braces against past,
        present, future—at the same time.

Love slices her perfect foot
        in half ("like the curtain in the Temple
split when Jesus gave up the ghost").
        But she doesn't complain or seek credit
for her morning ritual.
        She simply slips her left foot into
the other expectant slipper: A Queen
        who reigns over a universe of Sunday slippers & self-sacrifice.

Some praise her for her allegiance
        to bleeding out for complete strangers & their lazy respect.
Others, who live and thrive because she lays
        her life on the line each day—don't bother to learn her name.
She gets that her service requires eternal overtime
        & she'll never earn enough coins to rent a decent hot comb.
Banging her head against Lead Belly's naked squall,
        She lives for Phineas Newborn's refrains,
flowering on her morning plate.

Malcolm X

If I'm down today, I'm up tomorrow.
You can never keep a good man down.
You got a cup of sugar I can borrow?

Pull up a chair. A glass of merlot
To add to our flow & conversation?
Down in the dirt, but rise with doves tomorrow.

I don't care how long you cry and crow
About how life is treating you, Brother.
Keep a bag of sugar for others to borrow.

Don't be fooled. Ain't no free, easy dough
To be made. Roll up your sleeves; put the work
In. Down today but you'll rise with eagles tomorrow.

I know it's hard for you Brother, that every deathblow
To your stomach can weaken your knees, but stand up.
Sugar & light sweeten the hood, even a cup borrowed.

White men are assumed competent, but my ten-inch 'fro
Means I'm incompetent—before my interview begins.
I could be out tonight, but I've restocked for tomorrow.

It's a crying shame that racism has leeched very slowly
Into white pulpits. No wonder white pews fail to reflect
Or produce the sweet fruits of God—no light or growth.

If love fills us and we share it, there'll always be an escrow
From which we can double dip, when your patience dims.
We're down today, but we can brawl, relentlessly, tomorrow.
Friend, I have seven cups of sugar you can borrow.

Pitching Quarters

For Daryl Brown

Posting Up—between luck & wonder—
We stand before our cinderblock wall.
That is emboldened between the boys' and girls'
Bathrooms of our summer park. We believe
Lifting cinderblock & shaking an omer of iron
Onto our tongues turn us boys into men.

We know society's rules now
& who can piss on these same rules.
Without consequence. How to kiss your girl under
A new moon. Until stars convulse
In their purple pockets.
We've perfected our own groove,
Joined in the hips and backs of R&B.

We've learned the difference between
The Black church and the White church.
Between human compassion and White
Christian Nationalism. Who sips the red
Kool-Aid dripping from the loins & lips
Of Jim Crow: He pours a repulsive cup.

We are jammed with the fact that White
Evangelicals are empty brass vessels.
Preaching a gospel that never stirred
In the mouth of Christ or His disciples. In
public, you sing songs about His rugged
Cross. But, in your hearts, you lynch us.

You survive on a theology that maims us.
You hate our Jewish brothers & sisters.
Standing at the foot of Christ's cross
You hold our hands as if we are lovers.
It's as if you don't understand that He
levelled the ground before His cross.

Your twisted ethic (cloaked in honey coats and
Republican loam) never applies to you & yours.
But you expect me and mine to follow your law
& lucky charms to the letter. To adopt it as our
Own salvific alert & repair. What fool would
Sip an ethic that he has not written or sanctioned?

Severs our limbs with their lips/bibles
& private federal policies. Or they follow us,
Cloaked in Jesus-veneer & smiling arsenic smiles.
We have learned to look beyond your arsenic
Smiles & slanted logic. Your purpose & intent?
Either to erase our footprints with brooms
Of White theology. Or, to embroil our innocence
& fingerprints in contrived investigations of your
Flavor & bitter font. (*Brothers, don't sip the Kool-Aid*).

Standing before our cinderblock wall
(King of our July & our holy relevance)
Weighted with pockets of quarters
That could tilt chance's gold bucket
Our way. We take 12 holy steps
From the wall: It's Daryl's turn:

He toes a thick line drawn in red clay.
His pockets swelling with our quarters.
Turns his red baseball hat 180 degrees.
Before him ... six quarters, ill-tossed,
Flounder short of the cinderblock wall.
He pitches a quarter from his narrow

Right hip. Our eyes embalm every flip
Of his quarter (*"If this ain't devil's work
I'd eat my shoe and your shoe too"*). As if
it belonged in each of our mile-deep pockets.
His quarter, a single-winged bird with
no nest, lands, slides, kisses our Wailing Wall.

Elegy for Clara Williams

She'd been told to burn a grassy field
To prepare fallow ground for planting.
She'd never favored fire's selfishness.
Striking the wooden match on its box,
Clara walks along the edge of the field.
A Spring breeze quickens the flames.
She had not seen her sister, Helen, who trails. An
angel brushes a wing across Clara's heart. Smoke
burns her eyes. She turns on a dime.
Helen runs toward her in a dress of alarm and fire.
Clara beats back the flames with her arms,
Which begin to melt into one failed battering ram.

She walks a mile in her sister's shoes.
She walks a mile in her sister's shoes.

I watch her at her white stone churn,
Plunging a wooden paddle into milk.
Over time, her fingers created grooves in the handle:
Golden butter beads, gleams, only for her silver spoon.
One day her favorite slip ripped & her churn split
Down the middle (*"like the curtain in the Temple
rent in two when Jesus died"*).
The next second, her husband June dropped dead.
She wonders how to raise their eight children,
A woman in a spastic world of mean-mouthed men?
She reminds God that He had parted the Red Sea
With His thumb so His children could cross on dry land.

She walks a mile in Moses' shoes.
She walks a mile in Moses' shoes.

Clara's skin—darker than black licorice.
Darker than the coffee she percolates.
But she drinks it straight, black.

No cream, no milk, no sugar, no vodka.
Her arms are as thin as reeds,
But stretch tall enough to hold
Her eight children. She told me God had
whistled through her bones to stretch them.
I asked which particular tune God had whistled
To lengthen her bones—she could not remember
But recalls God had loaned it to a nightingale
After her lover had flown away.

She walks a mile in a mother's shoes.
She walks a mile in a grandmother's shoes.

So she leased land from White families.
Sharecropped cotton, cotton! Seeded
Mile-long rows from the levee to heaven.
They hoed cotton, pulled corn, chopped,
Weeded, picked, banked sweet potatoes in straw,
Pickled, canned fruit, squeezed heaven's sweet nectar
From sorghum & sealed it in silver tin cans.
By 1968, hard work had started bending her back
Into an eternal rainbow. She bought a pink Bluco
Radio after her last crop. Watched 33 grandchildren
Dance from her front porch, across the land by 1999,
Beyond the strobe of her eagle-eyes & caul.

She walked a million miles in a sharecropper's shoes.
She walked a billion miles in a sharecropper's shoes.

Bebop

Swinging in the afterglow of Genesis.
St. Creative Process propels Coltrane
A hundred years beyond his quartet's
zoot-suit swagger to conception's house.

The air in the Savoy is hoarse with *My
Sin* perfume. Dancers leaping miles into
The vault of stripped melodic chords. Saxes
Ignore tried & true to try true revolt.

Yet thieves lurk & grab in this Temple of
Improvisation. With unclean hands that
Steal, repackage & sell Coltrane's gifts of
rapid-fire fingering & eternal brass words.

Thieves—Miles Davis turns his back to them—who
Peddle his gifts across town for triple the price.

**

We live in a country of thieves and kings
for profit. Huddled round our quarters &

dimes. Pinching our pennies, nickels, dollars
until our currency squills, thins. But oils white

pockets in a holy flurry of proverb, contract,
ethic, cultural privilege, green greed:

"If you have no talent then steal, package,
resell another's bop-and-grind 'cross town!"

What if Coltrane & Dizzy had withheld brass
Wonder & melodic jaunt? What if these

Cool cats—gigging/blowing on the world's stage—
had iced their gifts & rebellion in maternal kitchens?

But Coltrane bops from my radio all day. While
crooks carve his sax in sixteenths & yawn.

***

A Love Supreme crests the Memphis vista.
Where Little Milton's piercing tenor reigns.
Next door to Big Momma Thorton's hound dog,
Panting to pay Graceland's mortgage & myth.
Elvis gyrates his narrow Mississippi
Hips across the Stage of privilege and
Reinterpretation. He knows the R&B
Jazzing his listeners is not of his blood.
But he's not the first to loot our ethos.
Stacking dollars, talking smack about his
Kingdom of Billboard hits & vinyl rock 'n'
roll. This King of ear hustling & bell-bottoms.

While our artisans spin their later years
Chomping government cheese & crackers.

****

Grooving in the heaven of high-hat patina,
Music grifters lurk for your milk & craft.
Beboppers of zoot play so doggone fast
Their eloquent fingers almost catch fire.

Listening to machine-gun melodies climb.
Take flight in a gust of revolution, scaling
Segregation's Tower. Which has enabled
Jim Crow to reign supreme with *their* Christ.

These melodic soldiers are not gigging
To clown or to entertain music robbers.
Step-and-fetch-it is not their creed & core.
Does not hold their feet to racism's fire.

No. No. No. They live to erase evil's footfalls
One lyrical chord change in holy phrasing.

Villanelle for My Morehouse Brothers

Life ain't no joke, but you gotta live it anyhow.
You only have one life to live so make it count.
Play hard or go home and lick your wounds.

If you make a mistake (*don't wilt*) you can rebound.
I once made the same mistakes seven times but
Life ain't no joke and you gotta live anyhow.

Each error is a golden arrow for your bow,
Releasing into the universe your single-minded
Quest for your reward having played hard.

You can't listen to someone without a single card.
But peep those who have lost big in the game
Cause Life ain't no joke but you gotta live & thrive.

You don't need much, my friend, just a sliver
Of Hope can drive your chances for success.
Or play soft, go home & lick your mistakes.

Not me! I'm roaring ahead—no time for half-baked
Ideas from a cupcake with no skin in the game.
Cause Life ain't no joke & you gotta buy milk & pampers.

Ask James Brown exactly how much torque
& skill it takes to come out on top in America.
Where colored men work harder then head home.

Dr. King advises us to keep working hard & live right.
Keep reading! Keep encouraging! Keep learning.
Don't be a loser, advising young men to give up the fight!
Play hard! There's no time to lick your delicate wounds!

Lindy Hop

No Harlem floor is safe from Coltrane's vamp &
draw. Let alone dancers whose sky-scrapper skills
Swivel between gravity's jealous embrace
& Spectator shout-outs, "How high can she fly?"

Well-heeled, with box-spring calves & lyrical
Footwork. Teaching time to mind its own
Business & onlookers with concrete blocks
For feet to sit & watch Willie Mae Rooker's

Skirt mushroom truncated chords & marvel.
As Leon James catapults her into the arms
Of "She Ain't No Joke!" & "That Girl Got Wings!"
I sport mismatched brogans from here to there.

Between abbreviated breaths & stroll
They trumpet *cool* with callaloo swing.

**

There is no ceiling his groove & moves respect.
Whether the *Cotton Club's* plaster and thunder-roar.

Or the *Savoy's* melodic beams and crushing growl.
He'd practiced in his mom's tummy with boom.

Hitting the dancefloor for the first time was
Not Leon James' first fast-foot rodeo &

Glide. Seems Lindbergh had eye-hustled a hop
Or two, jumping the Atlantic with gusto-skip.

Could you match Leon—point by lyrical point—
In a fusion of jazz, tap, Charleston &

Breakaway? Pivoting between kitchen
Rehearsals & an eight-count Jubilee?

No New York rooftop absorbs how Lindy
Scales melody's wall without one stair.

After Reading James Baldwin's Open Letter to his Nephew
For my niece Journee

... proud that she navigates
A kitchen of knives, nails, "Don't Touch That!"
& a grumpy garbage disposal—all alone. Only
Two. {Next, she will conquer the Big Bedroom

Beyond her granny's steep threshold,
Where silent stones are silver quarters,
Where trees anchor rolling grass carpets,
Arthritic limbs shoulder mockingbirds & stars.}

Today Journee stands before me, dutiful student of quarters,
Stars, birds & oak trees with wooden shoulders.
She stares at my forehead and her two-year-old lips
Begin to move. Silently reads my wrinkled brow.

Within my folds of flesh are my secret wounds.
I don't want her to read those bloody words of worry:
Not the horror stories of law school, but the day I graduated.
Not the lethal words of White evangelicals in seminary

But the day God pressed my tin ear so close to His chest
That I could hear His heartbeat: *thump, thump, thump.*
The next moment a thunderbird started pumping, pumping,
Pumping its wings inside the apartment of my Tennessee ribs.

I don't want Journee to read how a White cop had knelt on
George Floyd's Neck for nine minutes. As if he was kneeling on
a bag of beans or flour. But that a world pumped its iron fist into the air,
Demanding we be treated like the kings we are: imperfect, reaching,

Stretching (nearly translucent) towards perfection's warm, firm hand.
I don't want her early journey in our America to be ribbed by hateful
Words spewed by hateful people. Let her fly! Let quarters transform
Into goldfish in her hand. Let mockingbirds repeat "You Are Beautiful!"

Let her walk beneath a sheet of rain with no shoes or socks; head raised
Toward the sky. Her mouth gapping wider than a mason jar, receiving
Drops of Grace, kindness, mercy, love, patience, deliverance,
Power, faith, courage & affirmation into her Negro body.

Zoot Suit

The metal chatter & backfire of world wars
Won't dull the scissors or snap the needles of

Louis Lettes. Hunkered over a male pattern
He'd filet from bolts of cloth & black comedy.

Red butterflies (wings splayed from Memphis
To Cab Calloway's repose & woolly rations)

Seeped into Lettes' dreams in a gust of lapel
& high-waisted revolt. Big-shoulder ideas—

In the context of war ration & relief—
Don't respect the minimal leanings

Of White Privilege's Paternal huff &
Arsenic cough. Poisoning air, freedom.

Lean into this wide-legged day without
Regret, vying for a tailor's thread & juice.

**

Shimmering amid the textiles of slave
Code and fake White patriotism. Zoot is

Cool & kool is holy zoot. Zig zagging from
Chitlin' Circuits to Dizzy's fusion of

Field shout & revolution. Trumpeting
Standards to the tips of their toes. Saluting

Liberia's flag and Ma Rainey's dusty
Caboose. As she shouts "Ride my rails, Baby,

To the sky & back into my brown arms." Why
salute Jim Crow's flag of separate and

Unequal? Whose oral rinse blends
Hypocrisy, urban myth & police cover.

Rewrite this country's unholy truths with eyes
Narrowed by fact's frame & tapered trousers.

***

Blowback of White paternalism & unhinged
patriotism sporting a woman's flared
skirt & long faux fox coat. Singeing the nose
hairs of colored men. Who walk out Saturday
glow & bebop's holy heft, trigger & bounce.
We smell those arsenic breaths of police,
uncivil civilians & preachers. Claiming
our pomade, zoot suits & pocket-watches
(tethering us to rebellion, back-talk,
beauty & folding money) prompt police,
billy clubs, bricks, bottles & raised White fists.
Killing innocent men without provocation.
By the kilt & ragged yard, mobs traffic
under police cover & bigotry's tutelage.

Small-Pox Blankets

> *"I have never called a white man a dog, but today..."*
> Four Bears, Mandan Chief

Lakota, Cheyenne, Blackfeet, Four Bears,
& Other Saints of the plains & forests,
Swaddle their babies in the safety of
buffalo-hunting & teepees. Spiraling
from smoke to sky to star to warrior
Room of eternal bone/raw honey &
bloom. They ink & scribble clean history
on buffalo robes. Beyond epidemic's sweet
tooth & lethal terms, stalking lives for coins?
Yet, their White Jesus (reclining on a
Bed of White supremacy) twirls the day.
Combing blond heads & squaring blue eyes.
Offering sweets & salvation's smallpox blankets.

Jim Crow, absent backbone & bleeding heart,
Breaks upon thunderbird curse & payback.

War Room

> A.G. Gaston Motel, Room 30
> Birmingham, AL.

King and his soldiers huddle over hot
fish plates, iced colas, light bread & black resolve.
Elbow to elbow, beyond the murmur
of camera flash & blind White preachers.
Who have refused to follow the urgings
from the Holy Spirit so long that their
White hearts have calcified into gristle
& loot for a certain swag and swank.
Yet, King and his preacher posse pin their
hope on an empty cross—never emptied
of its dynamite & ragged lure: The ground
at the foot of His cross is grace-levelled.

If we jam our ears & dim our minds, then
no light can illume to show us truth's way.

***

Dogged prophecy and concentration's
curse brought them to this ragged table,
stretching from "Let There Be" to Bull Connor's
front porch—bonded to evil's jealous allure.

King and his crew know they're in the thickets
of this red State. That bends, flips & brawls when
Jim Crow flashes his mossy teeth. Blessing the
demonic twist & turn of White pulpits.

Yet in this hateful place children line up
to face down Connor's dogs & police dogma,
staring into the metal eyes of firehose
nozzles & separate-but-equal's lies.

There is a table loaded with the fruit
of the Holy Spirit that can redeem us.

Widow Maker

Highway 64 is the umbilical cord funneling us to Memphis from farms, nuzzling blues & balm. Before the rolling interstate system, this county highway was two lanes of risk running east to west. Highway 64, our widow-maker, a self-published "Treatise on Carnage & Consequence." Claiming & stacking *over corrections* inside and outside its concrete lanes: Men die. Women. An infant frozen by indecision: whether to cleave to the brown areola of Saturn or clear his sinuses? Then, he parts his dry lips …

This highway claims Negroes. Whites. A farmer trucking first fruits to Memphis on a flatbed truck (which doubles our hearse) miscalculates a hair-pin turn: eggplants addle, bushels of purple hull peas uncrate themselves & transform into spud missiles, writing their nutritious names on the windows of oncoming cars, trucks, vans. His truck flips so many times, *they say* the angels in heaven stop counting. Highway 64 works triple time without seeking one cent of overtime.

With no "flatbed hearse" to deliver our final fruits to Memphis, we enlist the Egg Man to drive our people—when he is not wolfing or selling eggs. As noisy as he is nosey. An egghead but kind. He carts clutches of double & single yolks to eggless Memphians. But Highway 64 does not discriminate & holds a grudge without compromise. It takes the blind. Hard workers. The godly & ungodly. Egg Man leaves Memphis one day, a pocketful of money and a new red silk dress for his wife. An oncoming truck stocked with lamb lumbers toward the city in a light mist; its driver, attentive to his cargo of hooves and wool & expectation but inattentive to his four, maypop tires cruising to Memphis. Distracted by a pebble in his right brogan, he presses his iron foot on the brake, the right rear passenger tire explodes & he fishtails in an oil spill—lamb chops & addled eggs take flight. A preacher, who'd just funeralized his father, spots lambs' blood raining & faints at his wheel.

Retort

"Don't worry about a thing.
    Not one blessed thing.
Come—have my seat.
    Remove your shoes.
What nice shoes you have!
    No scuff marks. My—what nice, rounded heels.
Slip into my fur-lined loafers.
    Yearlings surrendered their lives
So that I could walk on them,
    A gift from my heart to your feet.

I have a full leather set in my
    Bedroom (couch, hand-chair, ottoman).
I don't ask for much.
    Am easy to please.
But—I must warn you.
    I have a *humming jones*
for white powdery donuts,
    Nearsighted souls, slow-winded sorts
& other simple confectionaries.
    We can be friends—but I don't hold hands."

Uncle JP

Lift your head above the clouds.
If drunk, he's as light as beer suds.
Hope, released, screams very loud.

I've watched him glide into a crowded
Room with Nosey Nellies sniffing around:
He'd lift his head above lavender clouds.

He lived one life twice & never brooded
About the challenges he faced—homeless.
He'd learned hope kicked & screamed loud.

I've seen him push his shopping cart, pilfered
From the Piggly Wiggly. Holding his whole life.
His hope coils & springs above silver clouds.

Other homeless Memphians of your quarter bowed,
Regained strength from your dance & affair with wine.
They desire to lift their heads above funk & foam.

I never understood how such a proud
Man loved sleeping in the streets. Owned
A house of hope that cried very loud.

Maybe the seven rooms of your house held
You too tight, Dude? Your eyes too glued
To past mistakes? Hope in a wine bottle?

I can't recall how we learned
That you'd transitioned above.
You—looking down from clouds.
You, hope-soaked, passing a bottle.

Cow-Foot Soup

God sees everything you know. Everyone!
His eyes rove round the world and ping us.

Does not sport sunglasses or contact lenses.
Does not doze off beneath banana trees.

He sees us when we throw a rock and hide.
Listens to us destroy lives without reservation.

Knows our smiles are fake. Tongues, full of venom.
Pretending that we love who we wholly hate.

Why not be honest with ourselves, my friend?
Why sleep upon a bed of lies and lunacy?

Refuse to acknowledge White supremacy
Kills Black men for sport and ego-bliss?

Yet pray to God as if you are His child.
Who throws no brick, pledges no evil.

The Interview

How long does it take to shoe a mule?
        The farmer answers "five winks, seven winks—tops."
He compares shoeing a mule to shoeing
        The moon. The college graduate,

I remark that the moon is footless.
        "Have you walked the moon?"
No. But there is no mention
        In the current literature of the moon

Requesting a pair of tube socks.
        I'm sure. I've consulted the literature.
"Did you write those books you read?
        Do you believe words you haven't lived?"

Tiger's Milk

He prowls our streets in purple gators, a
Gold tip on each boot tip. Rousing pretext &

Reasonable doubt. Switching on our radios
That fill the airwaves of recent Black deaths.

Arousing us from soft beds, from feather pillows
Of self-regard. It's time for *power lifting*

& snort. If we expect change in this crumbling
Republic where racial profiling is holy scripture ...

Justice—if it's worth one red cent—destroys
The rock 'n' roll of racism & bigotry.

Kills the funk of Jim Crow judges that squill,
Piss under the scalpel of common sense.

Cease white *heehaw* steeping in cowboy hats
& white hymnals disguised as gospel truth!

St. Bluesman of Eads, Tennessee

Dad ladles lumpy oatmeal & flecks
of hope into our borrowed bowls.
As we sit at mom's perfect kitchen table,
listing toward Negro love & validation.

Dad is steady & heavy-handed.
Having shoveled sorrow & ore into
industrial ovens to flesh the moon &
wink at racism's slave codes & intent.

The plant's loud whistle signals that last
spade of ore & mercury. Asks Coltrane to
whisper "A Love Supreme" into
his home, leveling our tin bowls.

His heart swells with every whistle
and Coltrane's call-and-response.
But his paternal task must
be completed to ready us,

his six colored children. We
won't live our lives under
his tin roof, where rain
drums us asleep in his arms.

The Accomplice

Our mom is dad's eager,
Silent partner
In his parental *heaping*
Onto our thin-lipped plates,
Into our serious bowls—filled
With edible arrangements
Of African proverbs & "Don't
Do that round White folks."

Her psalms are emeralds
For our bracelets that we wear
Proudly, whipping winds into a fury
To defeat doubt & White supremacy.
Her scriptures are not bitter
For us, her testimonials & first fruits.
We are light & salvation for a country
Running drunk on White hate & idolatry.

But her psalms will need sweetening
("May, I please have a spoon of honey")
For those who refuse to acknowledge
That they benefit from racism's cancer.
We are the golden clutch for these two eagles.
Whose wingspans eclipse the snaking Nile.
Who shore up our shotgun house guitar,
James Brown's baseline & maternity's insignia.

We tabernacle in *this* shotgun house.
Our mouths are opened wide. Jawlines
Stretched by Expectation, awaiting her one
Proverb: "Don't believe a single word they say."

St. Improvisation Speaks for the First Time

"Fire's gutting this feather house!
Brothers, grab what you can grab & go.
Snatch the Tiger's Milk & cognac.
Forget that sheet music—
Brothers, take only what we N-E-E-D!"

America

Peace is your friend if you wanna keep pace.
Everywhere you go, some folk hate Black people.
My friend just caught a case.

I'm a Black man with a leather briefcase.
Brimming with Bobby Blue Bland records,
preaching peace into your house & space.

This country would love nothing less than erase
Every footprint we've left on land, sky, blue seas.
If Black people read a book, they expect a case?

I love my life & my gifts. I never wanna replace
The life that I've lived in this demon-filled country.
Cuz peace reigns in my heart; it takes very little space.

Listen, this is salvation: We must make sure Love outpaces
The evil of racism/White religious nationalism & Uncle Toms
Voting to destroy the Voting Rights of those who caught a case.

It's time to wake up and face the boldface
Lies White preachers preach from God's pulpit;
They don't want peace raining in our holy spaces.

They spend too much time disgracing
The Holy Spirit: pumping praise into
Republican purses, hate's briefcases.

America *could be* a great nation, a showcase
Of how God's love rinses our lives in lavender.
Where peace loops—sustains—because we make space
For her; she will stretch, purify, but never catch a case.

A Reliable Bridge

"I'd never met a poem until I read yours," says my mother, who stops at my bedroom door, cranes her neck into my simple room. I stare at my computer screen while my nimble fingers make *quick bread* of a few lines before they sour in my melon. I don't respond because I can't write & talk at the same time. "I never wondered what my words looked like on paper. Never wondered if they ever even had faces." She repeats, "I met my first poem when I read yours." A million linear feet of hallway separates her from my dime-store desk. She continues, "I could never talk on paper like that." As if repetition alone had ever built a reliable bridge. The hallway lengthens between us. "Until you, all the men in the family spoke only in wood—not words."

Jim Crow

He is their Jesus of partial salvation,
A totem crowned in the shadow of

White supremacy, religious lynching
& separate but equal. What a thing.

What a gizmo of minstrel showmanship,
Fleshed, girdled in the gore of poll tax,

Restrictive covenants and Republican
honor. What a creature of White religion.

What a utensil to bring to our buffet
Of creole seasoning, jazz & kindness.

Where love & acceptance spill over each
cup. Where compassion uproots evil's lair.

Bring your hungry here! We give them seats.
Lift your empty cups & expect sunshine.

The Potter

We think we know what makes the world go round.
We sink our teeth into this urban myth and bite.

Until its blood spurts across our tongues, lips.
Mortals, we think so much of ourselves, it's funny.

How can we bake *such bread* with so much pride?
We add, multiply, feign and come up short.

Our math is wrong. Our hearts are wrong, my friend.
Bread baked with so much pride will never rise.

I don't know why I do the things I do.
Or fall (face first) into a question mark?

I must confess sometimes I miss the point.
But it's okay because I'm not perfect.

Thank God I can fail time and time again
Without Hungry Eye counting each washout.

Stop-and-Frisk

In the funky trap of bigotry &
Loose cannons loom deadly, one-eyed blue beasts.
Hunting honeyed avenues, boulevards,
& streets. Prowling for sacrificial lambs

Under the pomp-and-circumstance of *Terry frisks*.
Black and Brown men walk out ordinary days,
Balancing the draw & release of deadly encounter.
We fall prey to this blue beast's theology,

Hardwired to bracelet me and mine—despite
That light and innocence infuse our lives.
Or that our hands live to lift our babies
Into the sky, guide them as they learn to walk.

The riddle between my freedom & *pat down*
Stirs an algorithm reason cannot balance.

Rooster Blues

Sweet Baby, don't wake me too early.
Let's wait 'til my rooster crows.
Don't shake me awake too early.   Sweet Ba—by.
We gotta wait 'til this rooster crows.
He crows once in the morning.
Then he won't crow no mo'.
Won't crow no mo'.

Woman, you know I work all day.
I can't play all morning long.
I work two shifts in an eight-hour day.   Sweet Ba---by.
So, I can't play all morning long.
Wait 'til we hear this rooster's song.
This bird's song will make me strong.
A feather song can make me strong.

Don't wake me too early.
Let's wait 'til my rooster crows.
Don't shake me awake too early.   Sweet Ba---by.
We gotta wake 'til this rooster crows.
He crows once in the morning.
Then he won't crow no mo'.
Won't crow no mo'.

My Straw Boss aint worked a single cent.
Working Black men like we're neoslaves.
Straw Boss aint worked one copper penny.   Sweet Ba---by.
(What if he should choke on that straw between his lips?)
Working free Black men like we're Hebrew slaves.
He may be the boss, but I got more money in my money-clip.
He's paid pennies to ride us all day,
but I got more dollars in my paperclip.

Don't wake me too early.
Let's wait 'til my rooster crows.
Don't shake me awake too early.   Sweet Ba---by.
We gotta wake 'til this rooster crows.
He crows once in the morning.
Then he won't crow no mo'.
Won't crow no mo'.

If you gone talk real bad about me, Sweet Baby.
At least let me give you the words to say.
If you gone talk real, real bad about me.   Sweet Ba---by.
(running my name in the ground)
At least let me give you the words to say.
My own words won't sting so much.
& I'll be OK. Sting myself a little—but I'll be OK.

Sweet Honey, don't wake me too early.
Let's wait 'til my rooster crows.
Don't shake me awake too early.   Sweet Ba—by.
We gotta wake 'til the rooster crows.
He crows once in the morning.
Then he won't crow no mo'.
Won't crow no mo.'

A Loaf of Bread

Lazarus Pool Hall... where pool had not been shot since his girlfriend, Osceola, caught Lazarus slowly grinding her sister's coffee on green felt & silver moonbeams. Master of his craft. He chopped the table into kindling, feeding the potbellied heater. Which squats in the middle of the floor, an eager student. Its black, iron stomach swells with each toast, tumbler of gossip or stick of dry wood it's fed. Smoke burns my eyes and coats my throat when its smokestack backs up & upchucks gusts of cypress, oak & hard truth. In the table's stead, Lazarus had hammered together a stage mined from cherry oaks, Memphis plywood, & tall cedars from Lebanon, resting on cinder blocks & second-hand theology. Tonight, swaying under a naked 100-watt bulb, bluesman Judah sips white lightning from a white teacup he brought from home. His hands, steady as a Singer sewing machine. The heater belches a cloud of oak & yeast-filled innuendo. Judah's voice rises, levels, then cuts away regret & shame, weaving us into a fragile bracelet of peace & patience. His voice is as clear as the glass of water I'm sipping. I hear tin cans, ghosts & buckshot rattling whenever he shakes his head. Moaning that his woman's love mixes with lavender to signal the approach of spring, but he doesn't own a loaf of bread to his name. Moaning that he can smell her sweet skin, but not feel her because triple shifts & a hard-knock life had calcified his fingertips into molten rock. Everything he touches feels the same: raw silk or sow's ear. Osceola, who owns every inch & acre of real estate in this sweaty jukebox, smiles & then sips warm beer from a jelly jar. Tells Lazarus to stoke the heater, which won't be satisfied tonight. No matter how much wood it's fed.

James Brown

Could stand on his good foot
cause he knew how to lay
a bad bass-line in the grooves
of black vinyl. Which outlives

a final spin of our turntable.
He called it funk but dad
tabbed it a man's juices.

How a man's funky juice
can stir a dance floor
into a sweaty frenzy
of energy is a good foot.

Brother Brown owned no bad foot
to get up on or shake off or
waste good funk on. Having never
spilt a measure of blue-collar sweat.

Flophouse

A place of hope triggered by guttural blues,
Lining bellies with seams of iron coughs…

Men broach her threshold with coins & cigs
To buy a loaf of holy bread & raw honey:

"Please bring me a tin bucket of love, Mam.
Pour your liquid spirit on my ashy head.

That's known no kiss in a million years, Lady.
So my head can shine like pure gold in the sun."

Queen of Minimal Amenities… We
Sleep in her doss house where dimes charm night

Into a labyrinth of shared bathrooms,
sage, close quarter & transient glow.

Ain't love Supreme! Ain't her hips high & round.
Slow-walking a trickle of men to strut & reflection.

Dutch Nigger

Club *Back-To-Back* in Eads rocks
Friday nights until Shaka Zulu rises.

Trades cowhide sandals for red gators
eating the skillful tack & sew of erasure.

We must write our own history if we
want truth to plumb the lineage of fact

& psalm. Otherwise, our gifts and talents
will be expunged by cunning colonizers

whose hands would erase Matzeliger's name
& leathery bloom from Patent #274-207.

**

A puzzle of 40 hours per week:
Leather, Negro survival & shooting star

rinses his day until it glimmers. Rises
above the funk & piss of White erasure.

Crests where St. Creative Process sharpens
Jan's pencil to a point of lead & prodigious

squeeze. His mind, a honeycomb of Zulu
Strut, Dutch tongue & tack and sew. Questions

and ambrosia whip Jan into
a frenzy of industrial light & Insight.

Before a Harney Brothers Shoe Factory.
Against White slur & jealousy's arsenic fat.

Hate, a united state of itself,
Kneels to love & reflection.

Osceola

Osceola, where'd you walk off to?
I've worn out five pairs of shoes trying to find you.
Sweet, sweet Osceola, where'd you walk off to?
Lord knows I've walked out seven pairs of good shoes looking for you.
I only got one pair left and then I'm gonna refuel.
Walking out my last pair now, then I'm gonna refuel.

My momma say I need to leave you alone,
That you ain't work one thin dime.
She told me to leave you alone (stop worrying about you),
That you ain't work one single dime.
Dad understands but believes you're not the marrying kind.
He understands, Good Lord, but don't believe you're the marrying kind.

Villanelle Dressed in Blues

If you're not careful you will learn.
"Come closer, lean in, loan me one ear:
If you're not cautious you will love."

Would you like me to be your cover?
A signet ring approving, protecting you,
Simmering in gin & clove as you learn?

Maybe lean back into safe arms, a surgeon
Of the heart knowing exactly what it takes
To be too cautious and never fall in love.

The truth is grit & glass slivers. Not a voice-over
Mimicking how the truth parses syllables, intent.
My friend, if you're not careful you will learn.

I need you to stand in the unforgiving light.
You're not perfect. I'm not. We must all earn
"That to be too cautious will cost you love."

Now that's behind us, we can each discover
Just how love can shine like gold in a bottle
Of *you were not careful so you are learning*.

It begins with words (though pointed) softening
In our mouths. Voicing words of encouragement,
building a home of honey and unconditional love.

If you're not careful you will learn
That we are starting something new:
We will not be cautious but live to love
Life's entirety, not just its low hanging fruit.

Phineas Newborn Jr.

He dreams red cardinals,
Feather Memphis skies.
Then red-headed birds
Spread wings so wide
The city skyline sags red linen.
Black preachers begin to think
Rapture's thread is binding souls
In good, good travelling shoes.

But Phineas runs, open-mouthed.
Fears his melodic fingers
Will feather & fly him beyond
His father's rule & mother tongue.
Then, what would he do?
Kiss around the sky for stars
During the day? Slow-drag his
Fingers across his ivory house

Of Swing & Improvisation
Until the Temple of Art Tatum
& Bud Powell chisels his name
Into its 57 columns?
He knows what he must do.
Push forward, even with his hands
Handcuffed behind his back. Hope will free
His hands & he will keep preaching.

Phineas' Bones & Blues

He learned there are different deaths,
varying degrees of absolute life.

That words alone can destroy any light
in his eyes, any sparkle. Once, God spoke life

over a valley of human bones: sun-bleached,
disjointed, scattered on the desert floor

for scavengers; there was no speech
save the sun's red eye opening a door

in a skull for a sand flea. Whatever
the sand flea knew he buzzes in a hole

where an ear once felt useless but never
complained. Ezekiel rimmed an ear hole

with his index finger for King Good Luck. God
breathed, bones rattled, sought kin & anodyne.

Alchemist

She has given spools of herself.
She does not have thread enough
To mend the yawning holes in her
Stockings, pooling at her swollen calves.

Her head is clear.
Eyes—searching.
Her heart is light.
Then, God begins:

Whistles a tune through an open window
In her kitchen; it rinses her mind & washes
The soles of her innocent feet. She walks
To the window and opens it wider.

This is how spring lifts winter off its hunches
To reclaim meadows, bends, rivers and Highway 64
(Stretching from the Plantation Inn Club in West Memphis
To the front porch of Phineas Newborn Jr.).

This is how Phineas, Memphis Ambassador of Jazz,
& "Smokestack Lightening" beefs on the keyboard.
His right hand is a trumpet. Left hand, a tenor sax
Monday, Wednesday & Friday. But swaggers & stomps

In baritone shoes & sweat every other day of the week.
How Phineas rinses his hair of metal shavings & grind.
How he makes a meal of purple plums & hoecakes of Swing.
Fanning his 10 fingers, wings of paradise & interpretation.

Art Blakey

On Friday nights rain drums
On the tin roof of our home.
Transforming our tin roof
Into Blakey's hi-hat cymbal.
As Blakey paces his *Jazz
Messengers* into a shower
Of improvisation & Swing.
He knows his way around

The stratosphere of a drum set.
If Blakey does not take a break
His sticks will ignite, burning
Proverbs of improvisation
& the creative process
Into our pliable minds.
Onto the tips of our fingers,
Stained purple from shelling
Mountains of purple hull peas
Into my mother's itinerant bowl.

Our fingers (kings & queens
Of shotgun house walls
& 14K faith) will march
Us into the stifling halls of men
& women who question our worth,
Intelligence "before" they interview us.
Theologians of bologna sandwiches
& systemic racism, these men & women
Stroll around their dank closets, fitting
My people with verbal & literal slave collars.

But we've never been slaves.
Despite their liquid constitution.
Despite their porous treaties.
Despite their empty religious rhetoric.

We've always been rebels.
Costing us limbs, tongues,
Feet, hands, eyes, ears (both),
Babies, husbands, wives.

So, Blakey drums on our roof,
His hi-hat of drive & Negro
Determination. Drumming
Stirring up our spiritual gifts.
His *Messengers* & hi-hat messages hull
Us out this raggedy Friday night.
Dad's pockets swelling with folding money
As our laughter lifts the tin roof one inch.

The Reluctant King

Look at his shoes!
You'd never guess
That his parents are
Cobblers for Christians
& insurance salesmen.
Consider the soles of his shoes!

He's tramped through
Every smoky shake-joint, church
& laundromat in South
Memphis. But still refuses to wash
The soles of his shoes, broadcasting
Phineas' sincere dislike of simple chords

& platefuls of pre-determined responses.
He didn't learn to tie his shoes on time.
Tripped over pencils, pens, paper.
His momma barely can look at him.
His daddy only looks at him on Mondays.
Would you loan him $5!!!?

I wouldn't loan him one thin dime.
Not even if Phineas begs me.
Even if Phineas offers me a gig
In his house band of lexical phrases & light.
Revving West Memphis gospel & Al Green. Phineas
Could offer me the man's shoestrings, tethering
Improvisation to Monk's black hat, but I'd still pass.

Phineas

He is no bigger than a pinhole—
        at first. Receives no front-page coverage:
He is never interviewed.
        Never headlines. Relegated to a life lived
in an iron footnote.
        He could calcify into desperateness & stone.
No one takes him serious. Not
        the pretty lady with the wide hips, sporting a gold
ankle bracelet. Not the sporting woman
        with one gold tooth in the center of her mouth.
No one takes him serious!
        This morning he'd considered running an add
in the evening newspaper.
        Rummaged in his pockets for folding money
& remembered he'd spent
        his last on aspirin. Never regaled his own reflection,

even though he's younger
        than Robert Johnson's blues. There is no mirror
in his House of Windows & Lingering.
        Which is okay because he is not vain.
His shoe soles never thin
        though he walks & never rides.
Owns a single silk pillow.
        Lingers at bars sipping stale beer.
He attends church only during
        funerals (Emissary of Grits & Regret).
He has no father. No mother.
        (Would you claim him?)
If ignored, he could lapse into stomach
        cancer. This morning he thought he'd heard a preacher
call his name; but he righted himself—
        only to see a dog hobble into the preacher's arms.

A Moment to Dress

The Sultan of Cracked Eggs & Used Hens' Teeth.
Not to be confused with those bums who thump
& coax microwaved messages from liquid texts.
To suit themselves & fasten us into eternal religious
straight-jackets. I have a lot to live up to.

But, I have no theme music. Not one simple note or
Negro chord progression to announce my presence or
My plain plans to restore a semblance of
Honor and loyalty to the Universe of
Freedom in this overgrown lot, America.

I don't have time to tinker around second-hand,
microwaved sermons & White coded messages
That extend pockets in gold, silver coins
& good folding money. At the expense
Of solid, sound theology that centers us.

As White perversions bark & threaten the Wall of Common Sense.
My friend, I don't have time to tinker under the hoods
Of White evangelicals who refuse to look
Into real mirrors & unpack what they see, smell, feel, hear,
Experience & think. Or the time to motor through impotent creeds,

Clustered church meetings or town hall gospels
Of pride & alleged supremacy. Good people, this is hard-nosed
Missiology (not to be confused with "messiology")
That I've been tasked. Let's go: White policemen are pressing
Their knees onto the necks of handcuffed Black men.

Expendables

We receive no front-page tutorial but
A flimsy word or two buried six feet

into an obituary's embrace & rumble.
Thriving within a bangle of *boom*

& bracket, we've made cotton king in America.
Our backs (blackboard & testimony to hate's

perfect pitch and gore) impart a fleshy
Language lecturing students of racism's

Heart & lurk. Yet our heads are raised to the sky!
We march! We fight! We shout! We listen still…

Free from history's iron footnote. Shaking
lose Jim Crow's xenophobic claims.

We thrive while others fall asleep in sorrow's
lair. Celebrating Negro blood & kin.

Turn Your Plate Down

She listens to Phineas Newborn's
"We Three" on vinyl. Sips from a porcelain
Teacup, two ice cubes float in an ocean
Of gin in the petite cup. Each revolution
Of the record on the turn table reminds

Her that her man has a lion in his pocket,
Shaking its magical mane into a red chitlin' bucket.
Cause the blues point her shaggy prince
In a million directions at the same time.
Let this lion lift his head and roar. If

The savannah of her man's pocket is
Deep enough to hold its deboning baritone.
Which clothes the Three Wise Men spinning
On her vinyl in floor-length cashmere coats
From Weber & Heilbroner. The men squawk

Improvisational smack through chunks
& clumps of passion fruit & chord change.
First chewed in the chamber of Paul Chambers, Phineas,
And Roy Haynes. These Three Wise Men focus
Their eyes on the same star & its tail dangling

Above the broad shoulders of Phineas' piano.
Ear-hustling the strings of Paul's double-bass
And the instrumental halo circling the universe
Of sound hovering around Haynes ("Snap Crackle").
Who'd dip his sticks in lightning before taking the stage.

Whenever Chambers draws his horsehair bow
Across the heart of his base, Hannibal would raise
His head from history's brutal footnote. Requesting
A porterhouse, a cold beer & 37 elephants to frame
The Roman battles beneath his bronzed feet.

Liturgy

Before the interview begins
They will assume we are not
Qualified. That we don't belong
Though we are bone & blessing.

Our college degrees are useless in
this slave collar of American insanity.
This is the killing floor Howlin' Wolf
Squirmed into a knot to unwind Truth.

You must ignore the spiritual handcuffs
Of White evangelical myth & license.
We are True Believers. Whose hope
Does not hinge on White notion & dope.

Gluttony

What must I smell & look like?
A sink full of rotten chitterlings?

My momma is Good-looking.
My daddy works three jobs

When some folk won't work one.
My folks raised me to work night

And day to dress my table with lemon
& light. Then, I'd be good-looking too.

The Idiot Who Would be King

He dines on greasy burgers & tailpipe
Fumes from diesel-grunting Conservatives.

Adrift in oily hours of navel gazing.
Snubbing good sense for cherry-topped sweets.

You cheat at golf. You lie when truth would win.
Ignorant of consequence's blossom & lure.

While telling the hungry they eat too much,
Babbling the homeless occupy too much space.

Yet, Trump stomps sugar feet on our offering …
Crushing republic bones of gay & straight.

Tracking religious hoopla from coast to
Front pew & from slanted pulpits to D.C.

Who dropped him on his curdling head,
The Reigning King of Bologna & Grudge?

American Proverbs

For George Floyd

WE
determine
if
you people breathe—
how shallow ... now deeper.

WE
decide
if you draw that next breath
into your black lungs for Black life.

WE
orchestrate/manipulate
on which blocks & on which corners
you may stand
& sing your raggedy blues.

WE
roll
our own loaded dice & decide
how you will die
& where you will die ...
Yes, when you shall die.

WE
weigh
your every breath & hope
on our pristine scales.
These economic decisions
do not concern you people.
You people can't really read.
Can't really write a simple sentence
without superior White instruction.

Tomorrow,
WE will begin
charging
you people for oxygen & light.
And unteach you how to drive cars.

The Statue of Liberty Meets Bessie Smith for Sunday Brunch

Lady Liberty: I have the crackers. Gurl, did
you bring the liver cheese?

Bessie Smith: Liver cheese!? Gurl, I thought
you were running things in this country.
Do I look like I got a meat grinder
between my thighs?
You better walk down to the corner grocer.
He'll grind what you need.
He'll sho'nuff grind what you need.

Lady Liberty: How much per pound?
Gurl, I spent almost all my coins
on a jar of pickled pigs' feet & a can
of camphor.

Bessie Smith: I paid fifty cents per pound.
Listen, while you placing your order
comb your blond hair
before he begins his grind
& he'll probably charge you one flat dime.
He'll sho'nuff charge you one thin dime.

Lady Liberty: Good idea. Can I borrow your comb?

Bessie Smith: My comb!? Gurl, you know we don't
use the same comb.

Steel-Toed Boots: 1965

White managers fire Black men in Memphis
(*on the spot*) if they suspect our men own cars.

So, father & his friends park five miles
from the car plant & hoof it to work.

But, an aromatic miracle blooms in each boot:
Cherokee Roses trellis leather heel to steel toe.

Requiem for a Lightweight

Today, he forgets his boxing gloves,
lost in a rabbit hole in his locker.
Owns two pairs but he loaned a pair
To a friend with feather-weight hope.
He can't enter any ring without gloves!
Can't competitively box a ringdove
Without the necessary foxgloves:
He would lose without one red blow.

How can he forget his gloves!?
How can we take him seriously!?
On a good day, he is Theologian to Moths,
Root Rot & Unreliable Returns. On a better day,
He forgets his trunks. His trainer, keeper of truth
& patience, pleads with him to abandon
Dreams of the ring & sell Girl Scout cookies
until he regains heavy-weight composure.

His mother blossoms in shame.
Tosses, turns, flips on her bed
Of engagement & strict rules.
Reminds God of her obedience.
She had never complained
When He shorted her no less than
135 pounds of blessings & peace.
Yet she remains, slugger of his word.

His sisters cry well into the night
Spinning from their tears a story
Of defeat. Written on their faces
So any fool with one eye can read.
Maybe if their single-bout brother
Slipped in a few kidney punches
("He's single-handedly destroying
The family's reputation"), or a head-but.

Now ... light weight with no gloves.
Who, more often than not, remember
His trunks only because he loves silk
Reaching up his muscled thighs.
Who is to blame for this light-weight
("I bet he can't even hold his liquor")
Standing before a cracked mirror
Hope streaming from head to toenails:
He has forgotten his shoelaces.

Ali in Full Bloom

He moves with style & grace upon the world
(Footwork that tricks the devil in his own game).
Every footfall is a student of R&B.
Gliding upon a ring of prophecy & time.
Flashing a smile, disarming men & women
Of bigotry & hardwired insolence.
A holy smile that lifts the gloom of doubt
From minds dimmed by history's false claims.
He was beautiful before he knew it.
Victorious before he gloved his hands.
Winner before he entered doubt's ring.
How strange a nightingale of his own song.

Don't let this country's hate consume us all.
Be Brave! Be Brave! Stand in the light & fight.

Villanelle for the New York Stock Exchange

For Rosie Smith

I fell in love with villanelles—seven times.
Our house is pitched on clover & love.
My momma got a giant black purse.

Have you found yourself immersed
(*Up to your eyeballs*) in possibility &
Seven villanelles with lavender bursts?

I never apologize for my animal thirst.
How quickly, knee-bowed, I offer thanks
For Momma's black patent leather purse.

This is the key: Brother, jump feetfirst
Into a rhyme that suits your heft & face
While falling in love with a vanilla villanelle.

Don't second guess. Don't jump headfirst.
Or plough into a messy plate of wonderful
Words that don't mean a hill of beans.

Square your hips toward Lead Belly's horizon.
Understand you have only one life to live (happily),
Treading in a loop of endless villanelle & liver.

Not everyone who you cross will forgive
My bravery, your grunt, our healing touch
Where Black moms carry solid black purses.

I fall in love with star-dusted villanelles,
Pooling in the heart of Rosetta Tharpe
& her guitar, posted in the vault of rock 'n' roll,
& the eternal, black purses of colored women.

Sonnet for the Boxing Bumble Bee

We take to the air without one clear glance
Buzzing around the world with no regrets.

Seeking the sweetest flower on its bud.
Cassius Clay floated round the ring on wings.

Packing nitroglycerin in each red glove,
Sealing the ancient art of *punch-and-cover*.

He calculates chance's three-minute draw
from a cosmos of 12 rounds and screams.

He is more than pugilist of poems and dare,
Floating on air within a square of hard knocks.

But an intellect of Truth's gruesome draw
Whose voice drums beauty with every swing.

He snares us with words of light, remedy & charm.
Assures Black boys who forget how beautiful we are.

Shade Tree

Under an oak with Chicago shoulders.
A tack-and-pulley singing
Dead-man blues for Memphis.
He extracts an oily motor
From the cavity of the Crashed
Ford: gut-splayed in a sea Of
Rosemary, sage & prospect.

He hunkers under the rusty hood
Of his uncle's former Ford truck.
Lost in the fumes of oil & fortune.
He'd purchased the grey truck
But plans to spray-paint her
Flamingo pink after he saves enough
(*"What kind of man curses a truck pink?"*)

His uncle had wrapped his metal woman
Around a telephone pole—wired for gossip & intel.
He had learned to remove motors from trucks,
Watching his father like a hawk since he was a boy.
But this is his day and his timing rules *this* pink hour.
Salty sweat streams down his forehead, a motor
Thief with perfect scalpel & perfect swing.

He wipes his forehead with a rag blessed by Rev. Ike.
Now, the really hard work begins. Work that separates
Novices who tinker around the fringe & foliage of horse
Power from authentic shade tree mechanics. Who'd raised
Pyramids from Egyptian sand and *what if*. Spinning
His baseball cap 180 degrees on his shiny forehead.
Plunges hands into the torque of choke & absolution.

A Lament for Lightnin' Hopkins

A dogwood accepts its annual cue, erupts in Linda LeKinff's volcanic palette of pink plumage. An ancient restlessness & longing for freedom. A Memphis wind stirs the dogwood's universe of pink, loosens early blush from its perfume & wooden follicles. Which float upon the flews & back of a lone black wolf, resting in a stand of dog rose, heather & China aster. This Black queen smells another she-wolf in sheep's clothing, seven miles up wind. Maybe the jealous-hearted bitch who'd pinged her location & howled to Old Man Winter her cellphone number & email address—he'd started tracking her last September—just as her breasts started to soften into butter and honey. She'd known not a minute's peace until this blossoming spring moment—sheltered beneath a sister tree of petal & wolfish pride. She has let herself go, again. Her hair is brittle and stands upon her back to be named, tallied & tagged. But she ain't no *everyday* bitch muzzling spring for the first time! In her heart pumps more lean years, hunger & hunt than she can count—beneath a horology of wolfs bane & clover. She rolls over, exposes her milky belly to pink petals & repose. Her mind dances between Hadrian's Wall & the back porch of Lightnin' Hopkins, crooning from his Texas doorway, "Lovin' is hard, Sweet Baby, but leavin' you is even harder. Lovin' you, Sweet Girl, is too hard a life for one man to stand, but thoughts of leavin' you stops my heart. Let's forget all this wrongdoing and begin at the start, Good Lawd, let's begin at the start." A whiskey still percolating deathbed blues near his right foot coughs & he kicks it with his *good foot*. His regular, everyday blues lace through this dogwood, seasoning every blossom, blanketing the wolf in a pink blanket. Lightnin's 12-bar blues transforms Mercy into a pup tagged Romulus, muzzling through the pink table of his mother's belly. Latches to one fleshy tit. Then, Lightnin's guttural, lowdown blues transform kindness into Uncle Remus, who fastens upon her other and (at that very moment) decides to live his life & thrive, even if it means salving minstrel oil & reflection on his muzzle 'til it shines like gold. The pups of prophecy and hard-grudges draw milk from their mother and spring by the mouthfuls. Like every earnest mother, she gives too much of herself until she's nothing but bone, hair & silky indulgence. Almost disappears with each sermon of milk & unbridled need drawn from her. She looks up through arthritic branches of the ancient dogwood. Closes her eyes & passes dogged hope through her prophetic milk: A city will be perched on a Palatine hill. A tiger will spray dog-tooth violets & hollyhocks on every hilltop & valley, marking his story in a Roman hour of alley cats & other milk robbers.

Vanity

"Stop munching so many plums.
Stop swallowing so many poems.
There'll be no obesity on my watch.
No portly bellies toeing *this* plumb line!
Look at your shoes! Your leather
Soles are never thin enough."

Please

for Kenneth Smith

Don't piss in my face
With state initiatives
& white nationalism
then call it water, my friend!

Don't draft criminal laws
That target me & mine.
While you & yours break
every law on the books
without repercussion or shame.

Hermeneutic

the shards in your mouth are not bone
not even related to bone
yes, they tear, reave, rip, rend
any person, any notion
any snub-nosed rhetoric
or theology not thought thoroughly through
but they're not bone

the shards, like your tongue, teeth, tonsils,
do not impede your speech
your ability to communicate
your ability to conjecture
respond, reload & surmise
loaves of connotations into tiny morsels, granular bites
like an unlicensed Baptist preacher

i've witnessed you remove
a person from his/her casing & cosmetic
next, you deboned the person's words
& watched a word's husk fall free … fit for the fire
then he/she & their perfected words stood before you
as dutiful students,
true bread

what causes you to pause are your daughters
"will they be able to speak with thorns
in their throats?" you ask
(your choice of words—"thorns")
no words rooted in the world suffices
explains your indelible you
you are a scaffolding of communication
& mercy beyond academic embrace

the shards in your mouth
are not bone, not thorns

not potsherd, not horns
not aborted expectancies
not skeletal by definition
but inborn
DNA's spiritual tickertape

Spiraling, speaking
in a single tongue
that breaks bread

American Theology

You'd always hated the color of my skin.
Without knowing my character or pause.

Sealed this public hate in private records:
Jim Crow injustice is your name or kin.

You lynched me from Popular Trees in Georgia.
Burned me (*alive*) in Tennessee and Texas.

This plague of hate stuns child & nature.
Spirals through centuries and staggers us.

But you left England just to praise your God.
To offer your faces to Christ for holy kisses.

To serve Him as waiter and cupbearer.
To live, work, die for Him without question.

How do we trust you as brother or sister?
As you've breached each treaty you drafted.

Elegy for Howlin' Wolf

My hairline has started receding
        to a cosmos beyond my care & counsel.
Ruining the possibility of dreadlocking
        my red hair. In a few years, I'll
be solely forehead & reflection.
        Not that I prize dreadlocks
more so than I'd prized my boyhood bowl cuts.
        Not that I would equate dreadlocks
with ageless appeal or like to lock my locs
        to plumb an Afrocentric center.
But wanting what I can't have drives
        me to regions of simmering regret.
This is a shortcoming. I admit it.
        But if your table is a welcoming table,
I empty my pockets of this shortcoming
        & lay it on the table. Alongside
your inclination to restate the obvious.
        You have made of repetition an art
exceeded by your thrift
        ("Save those orange peels! I'll dry them
& grate them in my Christmas cakes").
        Had I locked my locs earlier,
during my Morehouse years
        I'd feel more complete.
Humming in my own home—
        A full-throated blues. No cute flute
number. Backing Sonny Boy—
        As he breathed his every blue
intention into a borrowed harmonica.
        From the bottom of some river
in some state with no name (By now my tin ears
        should have fleshed).
New considerations should be for the young?
        New explorations are for those
who, having never failed, have no fear

       of flying. Of falling, headlong, over
the ravine with no respectable parachute.
       Wanting what I can't have revs me:
if there'd been no moon
       hovering in his tin sky,
Howlin' Wolf would have shouted
       until a red rose blossomed
into a room in his head & Mississippi shout.
       Cried for a truck he could afford
that hadn't passed through the sugary hands
       of seven lesser men; wailed for black brogans
that hadn't been worn by seven other men,
       with smaller feet.
I have other confessions.
       Some will cause you to
shake your head.
       Others will cause your heart
to stutter like a nervous child.
       I'm opening my palms
to you ("See, my hands are clean").
       I'm bellying up to your welcoming table
(sort of seasoned & sort of centered).
       This is my howling start.

St. Hummingbird

A mouth quicker than hummingbird wings.
Pumping the air until a hurricane awakens.

Ali, heavy weight champion of knockout & wolfing,
Undressing friend and foe with daywork & dazzle.

Howard Cosell, student of Ali's charm & swagger,
Was king of *Telling It Like It Tis* and stiff toupees.

Blow-by-dizzying-blow, Cosell disrobed racists
To their knickers and stiff-necked theologies.

Despite these two heavy-word champions
Whites still profess Christ's cross & holy living

In 12 rounds of hollow love and failed initiatives.
We've spent countless years tallying your crimes!

Imagine a hummingbird's wings pumping air,
Raising a tsunami eclipsing heart & head.

Struggle

Don't fake it! Make it!
My first-grade teacher hates Black boys.
A grain of hope keeps me straight.

She judges we're all salty half-wits,
House-sitting in her white tea parlor.
Don't shake it! Break it!

As if we're strangers in her cockpit,
Waiting to be dropped on our heads,
But a speck of hope keeps us straight.

"On a good day you're deadweight."
"Why not try to be a credit to your race?"
Don't freeze it! Roll it out & bake it!

She treats me like I'm an inmate.
Her blue eyes pin me to the wall,
But a crumb of hope keeps me strong.

Black boys stand on one foot for one hour long,
In the back of the room, sweating a gallon a day.
But she won't break us cuz she didn't make us.

We are young, Black lions roaring seven centuries strong.
Risk beatings when we whisper correct answers mouth-to-ear,
Along our invisible chain gang on the back row: *We got this*!

We take a brother's beating cuz we don't fake it! We take it:
Across our shoulders (*Leadbelly's horizon and gritty resolve*).

Or down sturdy, short legs reaching from thunderbird to ring
Shout. Here, a mustard seed of hope stirs our hearts to sing.

House Money

Where catfish trend in hot grease & raw jazz.
Born from a line of backbeat & shake-joints.
Where beautiful women in high-waisted jeans
Pose against a backdraft of choice & "Jesus."

Born to a flex of men who bronze & nuzzle.
Who sprinkle sea salt on their tongues,
Preserving proverbs before dressing
Us to face those who hate us. Stir us

In America's vat of Jim-Crow junk & lunacy.
Where top-dollar is paid to the most
ignorant & unlearned. Here, books are burned
by those who do not read & cannot reason.

From childhood to this feverish moment,
We learn to swing wide but with focus.

Critical Race Theory

I should be a broken man but I'm not.
It's a crime to be born Black in America.
Believe in yourself, even if others don't.

Black men are truly hated here: one simple grunt
Is considered credible evidence of terrorism.
We should be broken men but Lord, we're NOT!

We don't doll up in white sheets to confront
& lynch innocent men, women & children of color.
Believe in the truth, even if others don't.

After church, we don't self-deputize. A stunt
To please dark angels circling your mental sky.
Our women should be broken but they're not.

Then, head out & concoct a lie for a witch-hunt.
Seeking one who is harmless as fodder for fallen
Angels. Who *sift* you like flour & bleach your teeth.

We don't burn White churches as a racist stunt.
As an ugly joke to be shared at family feasts & dinner.
Our babies should be broken but they're not.

Let's be blunt: Consider your evil ways. Don't punt
This to the next generation of Americans. Confront
Your hate & love everyone, even if others don't.

Understand, my friend, hate respects no border:
It will take seed in your mind, heart, home & word.
Or keep trying to destroy us, but we won't be broken.
Believe that love uproots hate, even if some don't.

Desperation

He rambles around Memphis.
Without a single tooth in his head.
Nursing a faithful headache.
There's a steady pecking between
his good eye and his bad eye.
As if a red-beaked woodpecker
tapped bird-brained notions
into his tired, brown brain.
Drilling for worms & honey.
No remedy for his perfect migraine
(*And this is a good day*).

Seven Sundays ago, his girlfriend had left town—
with only the clothes on her back.
Her heart & mind had left
a year or more before; her body
had simply taken a later bullet
train: this scalding truth was the last
common bread the two would eat.
Still, he rambles this tired city in steel toe
shoes 25 hours a day. Almost
redeemed by shoe leather & drift.

George Floyd

In the orbit of a $20 dollar bill
& old hate. Floyd wrestles with White time.
He knows this arena, having quartered
In his skin & country forty-six years.

He'd walked the same tight rope (*heel, toe, heel, toe*)
all Black men swagger in the vault of White
justice, "I Can't Breathe" & White Male Ethic:
A black step at the wrong white time signals death.

Whites can breach the Capitol's walls with clubs
Of Trump-signal, privilege & Jim Crow's juices;
Their craniums crammed with hothouse gases—
Pumped by the *Idiot Who Would be King*.

A nation—driven by racism's demonic
Lure & one-sided justice—will implode.
In the greasy exhaust of illegal tender
& Derek Chauvin's demonic embrace,

buds a toxic romance of police-thunder
& "The Best Nigger is a Dead Nigger."

Eight minutes & twenty-nine seconds of
Handcuff, face down & *I Can't Breathe*

Signals & relays that black lives hang between
Face down, White-license & legal murder.

Had Floyd been a White man sporting privilege
(As if he'd nursed from Jim Crow's raisin-dry

Utters) he'd be sipping a chocolate malt
Under a Minneapolis sky—right now.

All life is precious to the man above.
Regardless of color, zip code, or swag.

Fall Face First

Into the mosaic arms
of Romare Bearden's
"Autumn of the Rooster."
Lick the lush greens & dynamic blues
of its small kitchen,
dripping onto the head of a white,
irreverent rooster. Who struts
the universe of this narrow kitchen.
Like a country preacher considering
an ancient text. While munching on a soda cracker.
Redeemed by every living word of the page.

The eye of a second rooster spots a bowl
of seven white eggs cradled in a woman's brown
arms. Whose hands are more whistle than meat
(*She is nothing if not tender*).
An empty skillet reposes on a wood stove.
Wishing for a crane's view of its narrow
Black life in lush, iron bloom.
The white rooster's second eye
Considers the senior couple. Autumn
peeps, shyly, through window blinds;
wonders how best to number its
slim days on Bearden's calendar.

Our couple is the color of tamarind tea.
Their bodies are soft, welcoming.
Their love for one another pierces skin,
invades each living cell & tabernacles
within the marrow of their colored bone.
They feel Spring uncurling, shyly, over each meadow
edging their years. Dressed in their Sunday Best—
(*In the middle of the week!*).
He sports his father's funeral shoes,
shining brighter than dazzle or daystar.

She can sing, full-throated, until the tin walls
of this Sugar House flicker.
Now that their children are grown;
(*She cut the final apron string today*).

They ruminate & cook together.
His biscuits elevate higher every morning.
Her grits grace each plate—
flavorful without bacon or butter.
They choose to eat from one tin plate.
Ignoring a division of fine china in the hutch
(Which holds up their tin roof).
Drink from the same simple coffee cup.
They've breathed the same air
so long they resemble one another:
He is her memory & she
completes his sentences.

Voting Rights

My friend, do you wanna win at the end?
Why do we quietly sit for evil & its hungry hounds?
Stand out! Why do you wanna blend?

Do we not know evil when he upends
The voting rights of the marginalized?
The voiceless? We can all win in the end.

Think about it: My people die of preventable
Diseases in the richest country in the world.
Afraid to stand out? Too easy for you to blend?

Read and question. Question and read. Let's expend
the time and care to lift and encourage. Never destroy
Our hope of making a difference at our ragged end.

This will take guts. It may mean that you reach, extend
Your hands to comfort those who do not look like you.
You can be afraid to stand out! Forgive but don't blend.

It'll cost you friends & family who will rescind
Their smiles and alleged love for you because
You've decided to stand out! Not live to blend.

You can no longer *turn your back* but bend
To make these years better than your past.
To love the least of us before you sniff your end.

Take a seat! Buckle up! This is not your dead-end.
Because you are stronger, wiser than those loud-mouthed
Fools. Who hate to see one red cent in our hands.
You're a lion now, roar in this arena of voter suppression & hate.

Shotgun-House Guitar

For Franklin & Florence Powell

An experiment of sorts. Self-imposed.
I lived a year without criticizing anyone,

Anything, anywhere. Checked my tongue.
Held my presumptions, points & diatribes

to miniscule numbers. Why, even the minimalist who
lived next door had been so pleased with my effort

that he smiled, shook my hand & pissed in his pants
—all at the same time. O' sweet fragrant success.

However, I had failed to consider a personal possibility.
While I had walked that year in a seasoned loop

(until the heels of my shoes had run over),
I had a lot of time to reflect/reconsider

& reload my personal construct. Which word
could I withdraw from rose & flint to identify me?

I was disinterested in the word's heft.
What one word best described me

when I was at my best (a giant-mouth
catfish dangling from brass lure & charm).

I was disinterested in a watershed of
polite discursive—veiled by self-interest.

I hankered for an irretrievable word that struck my soft spot,
a belly bloated & brimming with Leadbelly's used blues & cure.

Now, the minimalist (who is intoxicated by an algorithm
of Grind & Grit) responds in monosyllabic lines & terms.

Tempers our communications with guttural sounds
& elusive grunts. He would have hankered for the job.

Would have loved to separate me into parts/branches,
offering my heart & hope to repair dented harmonicas.

He'd place my Intent *here*. My reactions *there*.
My concerns in the corner. My salty failures in a cup.

Considered that I was a quiet person,
worrying a line until Ralph Ellison blushed.

My tongue tethered to hope by used guitar strings.
Though I'd applaud his effort & give him a slide

rule for Christmas, I'd reject the language he'd use to describe me.
Limited by his minimal leanings, he'd decline to consider my

Uncle Shadrack (for example) who had been eighteen
years old when slavery ended. He'd carved four posters

from cherry wood for his owners with kitchen knives,
but Shadrack had never slept a night in his own bed.

He had pilfered eagle nests for pillow down for others. But
slept on a pillow of chicken feathers & blossoming rage.

I sleep like a man who never expects to rise.
Now, I realize that words alone are insufficient:

A blue silk door without hardware.
Maybe just maybe I am pure sound.

What troubles me is how to harness my sound.
Grasp my perfect pitch though my ears are tin.

Maybe my tongue is pure alabaster.
Without echoes. Without discord.

How to harness the energy & power of it
without apology, without yielding my palm,

without being a gentleman about it.
I had heard that Leadbelly, (hankering

for a square meal of moans) had strung
six lengths of fishing chord to the side

of his shotgun house, slipped an empty
quart-sized mason jar as midriff & midwife

to his pain. He plucked this shotgun-house guitar.
Sung at such a feverish pitch that women listening

from their open windows (struck by the rancor & regret orbiting
their days) hung their heads & simmered, cried & laughed, wondered.

Their men, intoxicated by the weight of Leadbelly's words,
how his alabaster fingers made his shotgun house guitar

lurch & *talk back* in a flora of mustard greens & *Stick It Out*.
Watched & waited for their tin roofs to shine then levitate.

About the Author

Gregory Powell is originally from Arlington, Tennessee, about twenty miles east of Memphis. He graduated from Morehouse College in 1987 with a degree in Journalism. After working several years as a reporter in West Tennessee, he entered and graduated from the University of Wisconsin (Madison campus) Law School with a Juris Doctorate. He has been practicing labor and employment law for nearly thirty years. In 2004, he earned a Master of Fine Arts Degree in Creative Writing from the University of Alabama (Tuscaloosa campus), and in 2014 he earned a Master of Divinity Degree (Theology and Life Coaching) from Regent University. He is a proud member of the Omega Psi Phi Fraternity, Incorporated. Gregory has written several plays, including "Ruby's Harmonicas and Pianos, Incorporated" which was featured at the Black Theater Festival in Winston Salem, North Carolina in 2019, and is currently being rewritten as a screenplay. His poetry and dramatic compositions give voice to the voiceless and marginalized by opening a window onto social, political and theological blindness of contemporary American society.

Other Titles by Gregory Powell

Ruby's Harmonicas & Pianos, Incorporated (Lanham, MD: Broad Wing Press, 2019).
Tin Ears (Lanham, MD: Broad Wing Press, 2016).
Can be ordered directly from Seymour Press or on Amazon.com and Barnes & Noble.com

Contact Gregory Powell
at:
Gpowell65@gmail.com

www.ingramcontent.com/pod-product-compliance
Lightning Source LLC
Chambersburg PA
CBHW070118080526
44586CB00013B/1329